BOTTLE TOPS
THE ART OF EL ANATSUI

by **Alison Goldberg**

illustrated by **Elizabeth Zunon**

Lee & Low Books Inc.

New York

Text copyright © 2022 by Alison Goldberg
Illustrations copyright © 2022 by Elizabeth Zunon
LEE & LOW BOOKS Inc., 95 Madison Avenue, New York, NY 10016
leeandlow.com
Manufactured in China by RR Donnelley
Edited by Kandace Coston
Book design by Christy Hale
Book production by The Kids at Our House
The text is set in Le Mone Sans
The illustrations are rendered in paint and cut paper collage

10 9 8 7 6 5 4 3 2 1
First Edition

Library of Congress Cataloging-in-Publication Data
Names: Goldberg, Alison, author. | Zunon, Elizabeth, illustrator.
Title: Bottle tops : the art of El Anatsui / by Alison Goldberg ;
   illustrated by Elizabeth Zunon.
Description: First edition. | New York : Lee & Low Books, [2022] | Includes
   bibliographical references. | Audience: Ages 7-11 | Audience: Grades 4-6
   | Summary: "The life story of Ghanaian sculptor El Anatsui, a highly
   acclaimed African artist, whose tapestries made from repurposed bottle
   tops have been exhibited throughout the world"– Provided by publisher.
Identifiers: LCCN 2020057959 | ISBN 9781620149669 (hardcover) |
   eISBN 9781620149973 (ebk)
Subjects: LCSH: Anatsui, El, 1944—Juvenile literature. |
   Sculptors–Ghana–Biography–Juvenile literature. | Bottle caps as art
   material–Juvenile literature.
Classification: LCC NB1099.G53 A534 2020 | DDC 730.92 [B]–dc23
LC record available at https://lccn.loc.gov/2020057959

FSC
MIX
Paper from
responsible sources
FSC® C144853

For Akunz, Naa-Abia, and Belinda —A.G.

For Denny, an artist with endless vision —E.Z.

Acknowledgements
Thank you to El Anatsui for reviewing the manuscript, and for inspiring
this book with his extraordinary art. Thank you to Amarachi Okafor
for her valuable input as this book took shape. —A.G.

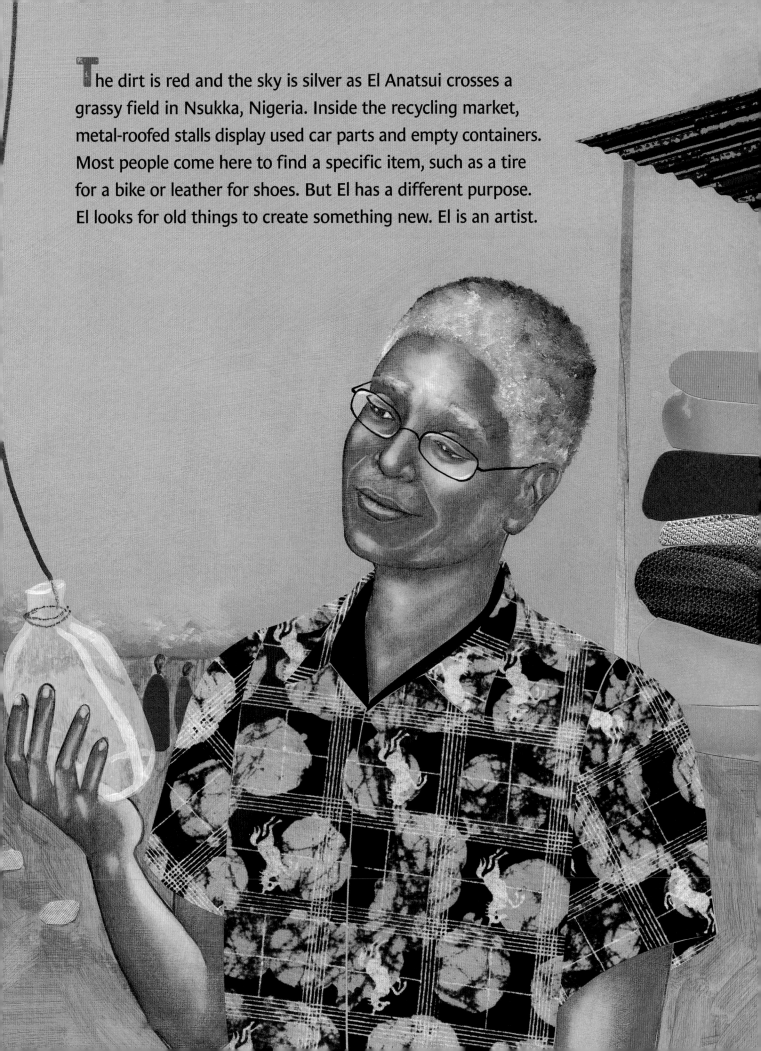

The dirt is red and the sky is silver as El Anatsui crosses a grassy field in Nsukka, Nigeria. Inside the recycling market, metal-roofed stalls display used car parts and empty containers. Most people come here to find a specific item, such as a tire for a bike or leather for shoes. But El has a different purpose. El looks for old things to create something new. El is an artist.

El has always written his own story—he even named himself El. The youngest of thirty-two children, El was born into a large family of weavers, fishermen, poets, and musicians. The town where his family lived was in a British colony called the Gold Coast. When El was very young, his mother died and he was sent to live with an uncle in a nearby town.

El wrote before he could read. Fascinated by the forms of letters, he copied the names he saw on doors. The headmaster at his school encouraged him with extra chalk. In art class El painted with watercolor, oil, and gouache. From an early age, he began experimenting with ways to tell his stories.

El was a teenager in 1957 when his country gained its independence from Britain and was renamed Ghana. With this new freedom, he felt a shift.

We could decide to do things on our own terms.

El went to art school. With no professional artists in his town, he did not know where this would lead. He was determined to find his own path.

As a student, El learned art traditions from Europe, such as plaster casting and drawing techniques.

School exposed me to what other cultures were doing in art. I was curious to know what my people did.

El visited the National Cultural Centre, which exhibited many Ghanaian art forms. Drumming. Dancing. Wood carving. Weaving.

Adinkra cloth, a fabric stamped with pictures that share ideas, made El think about how symbols could tell stories.

One image called *Sankofa* showed a bird reaching back. It represented drawing from the past. This idea resonated with El. He wanted to find a way to make art that could connect to the history of the people around him.

In 1975, El moved to Nsukka, Nigeria, to teach.

El searched for a material for his art and chose clay. Thinking about how old things could be made into new things, he used broken pots to make new ones—mixing ground-up pieces with fresh clay.

The new pot acquires the strength of the old pot—it's like the memory of the old pot.

El liked this idea of including the memories of old objects in his art. He saw it as a way to connect to the past. When the university's kiln broke and El could no longer fire pots, he looked for other ways to apply this principle.

El collected objects, particularly ones that had passed through human hands: milk can tin lids, old printer plates, broken cooking utensils, driftwood. He scoured the local recycling market. What other people saw as scrap, El saw as materials with a history—materials with the potential to become art. He thought about the stories these objects carried: Who made them? Who used them? Who had touched them? How could his art connect to those stories?

If you touch something, you leave a charge on it and anybody else touching it connects with you, in a way.

Over decades, El experimented with different materials and techniques. In wood, he made marks by gouging, sanding, drilling, and burning.

El tried a chain saw, which he found had its own language in the quick, straight lines it created. He made sculptures with parts that could be rearranged.

Each time El tried something new, he brought with him the experience of all the experiments he had done before.

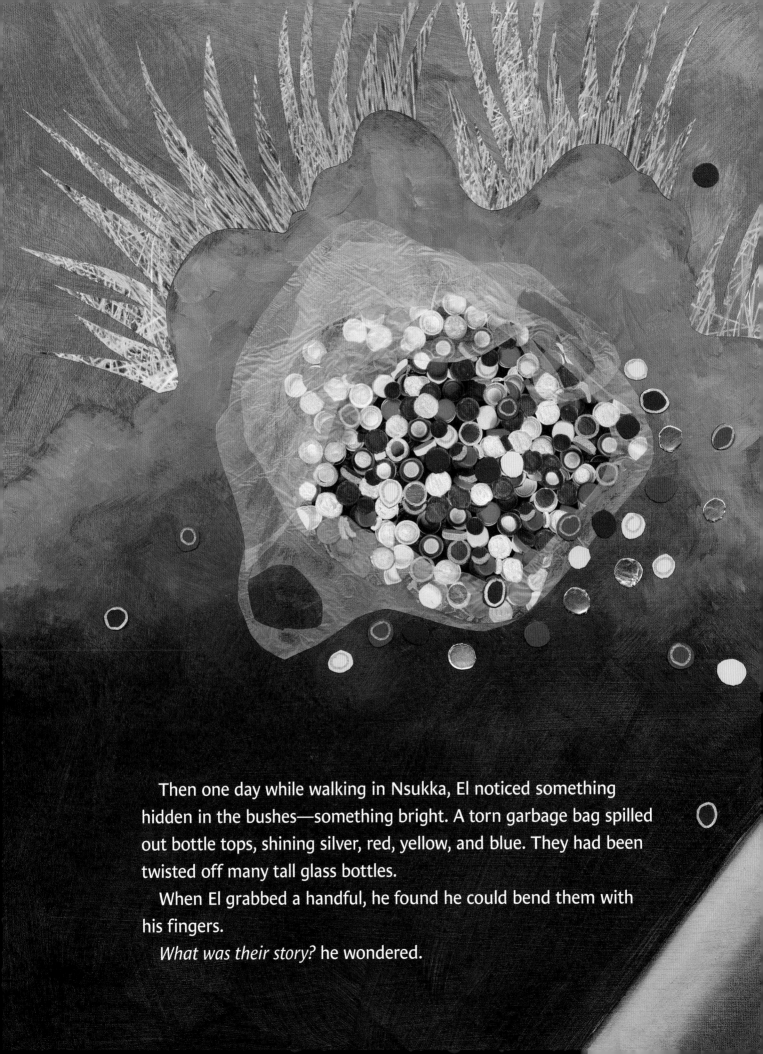

Then one day while walking in Nsukka, El noticed something hidden in the bushes—something bright. A torn garbage bag spilled out bottle tops, shining silver, red, yellow, and blue. They had been twisted off many tall glass bottles.

When El grabbed a handful, he found he could bend them with his fingers.

What was their story? he wondered.

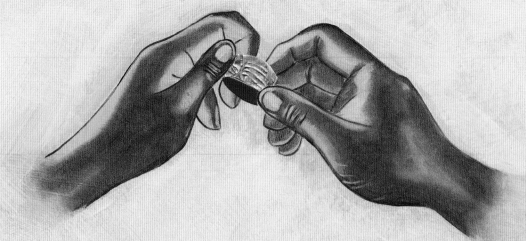

Inside his studio, El and his students tore the bottle tops open. Though the metal was jagged, they worked with their bare hands to feel the material.

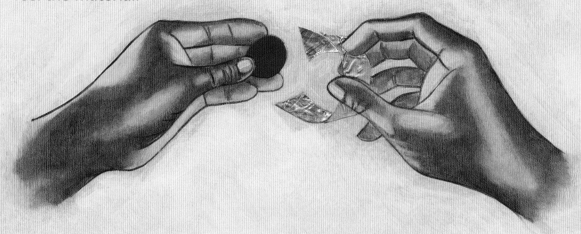

El separated the bottle top into parts. In the metal that wraps around a bottle's neck, he found a band.

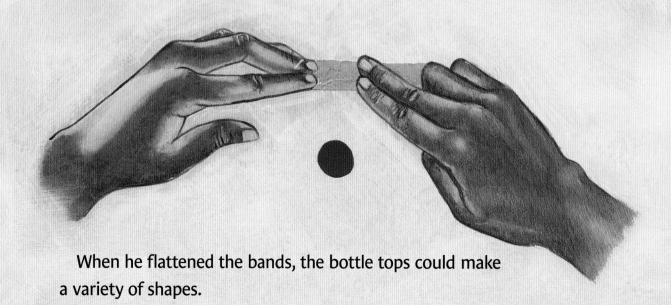

When he flattened the bands, the bottle tops could make a variety of shapes.

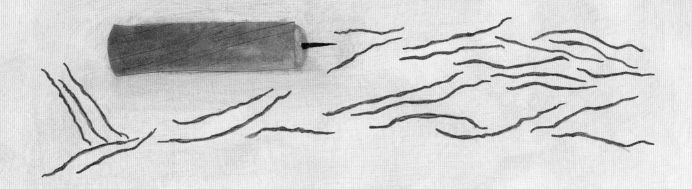

El punched holes into the pieces with an awl and used copper wire to join them together. Connecting the bottle tops in this way created a rough chain.

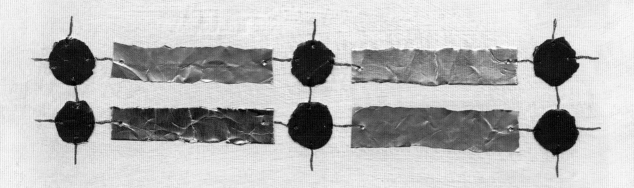

El fashioned his invented forms again and again. He made a large patch by attaching dozens of bottle tops together, using the wire like thread.

The patch was flexible and fluid. The bottle tops jangled and rattled when moved around. Some parts had words on them. The metal shimmered.

The idea eventually came to me that by stitching them together I could get them to articulate some statement. When the process of stitching got under way, I discovered that the result resembled a real fabric cloth. . . . The colors of the caps seemed to replicate those for traditional kente cloths.

El expanded on the patch to make a new type of sculpture. He purchased used bottle tops in Nsukka, and assistants helped him flatten, shape, and assemble the metal. As the artworks grew, he found ways to add texture and dimension.

El kept these experiments in his studio for two years. They were different from his other work. The bottle tops spoke to him, but would they speak to anyone else?

At last El folded and packed his new creations into crates, along with some other sculptures, and shipped them to a gallery in London.

When El arrived, he was surprised by the interest in his bottle top sculptures. Viewers were drawn to their unusual material and size. Draped on the wall, each one reached more than nine feet tall. Seeing his work displayed in the gallery and hearing the excitement about the sculptures encouraged El to find out what else he could make with bottle tops.

Soon, El's bottle top sculptures traveled to exhibits in New York, Dakar, Paris, and Tokyo. An enthusiastic art dealer invited El to participate in a special exhibit during the Venice Biennale—one of the most famous art shows in the world.

With the help of dozens of local young men who worked as his assistants, El gathered what he needed for the exhibit. It could take a whole day to make a single small patch, and El wanted hundreds of patches for the large sculpture he had in mind.

He scattered patches on the red-tinged floor. Some pieces were wide, some thin. Some textures were twisting, some flat. The colors were glimmering and bright.

El arranged and rearranged. He added new patches and took others away. He photographed each composition. He worked like a painter and a sculptor at the same time, considering color, surface, light, and form.

As he worked, El thought about history. Bottles like the ones these tops had sealed originally came from Europe and were brought to Africa by merchants. This reminded El of the transatlantic slave trade.

When I take a bottle cap and I cut it, I just have the feeling that I am working with the material which was there at the beginning of the contact between two continents (and eventually three continents). . . .

El thought about how old things could be given a new purpose. He had seen people bring scraps of fabric to the tailor to make patchwork—not for fashion, but because that was what they had. With bottle tops, he had found a material close to hand that evoked his history and environment. They had a past, and could have new meaning too.

At last he stitched the patches together like a quilt.

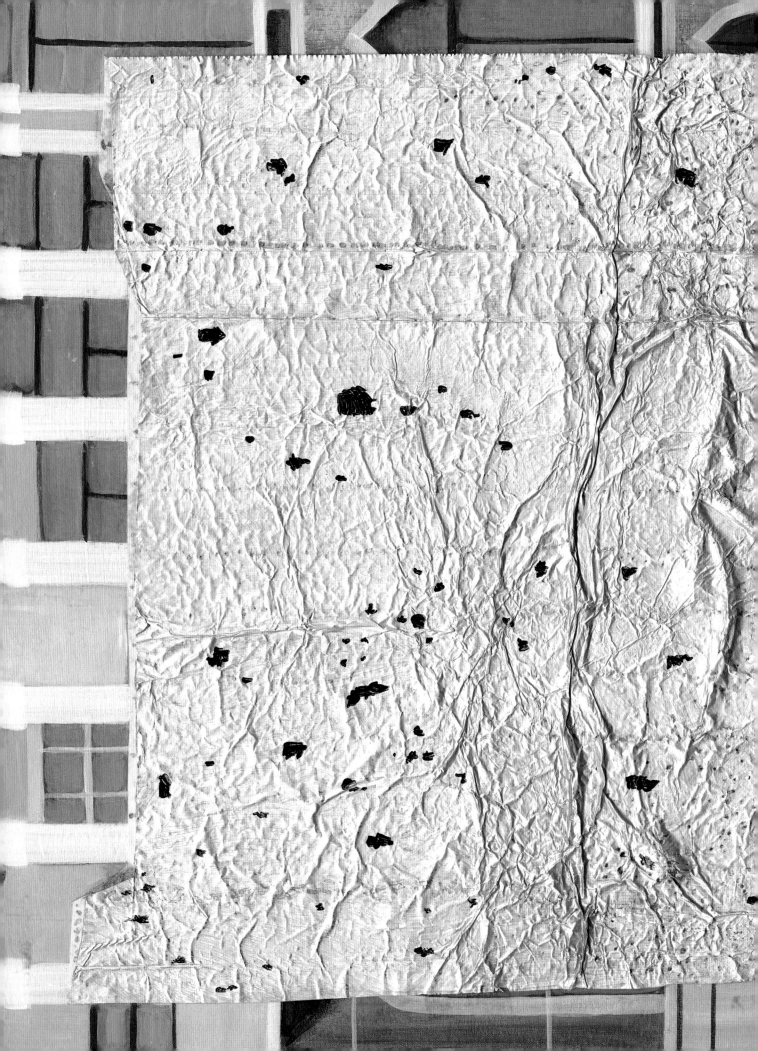

In 2007, El brought his bottle tops to Venice.

As he hung his thirty-foot-tall sculpture, he created curves to reflect the light and folds for catching shadows. He cut holes to reveal the building underneath. The sculpture wove together old art traditions and original techniques. Recalling history, and shaping the present. Attached, and flexible. El gave it a name: *Fresh and Fading Memories.* Viewers stood close, admiring the small metal shapes. They stood back, astonished by the bottle tops' transformation into an enormous, shimmering cloth. This sculpture was unlike anything people had ever seen.

Linked together, bottle tops can cover buildings. They can tell stories about history and culture—stories that link people together. Today, El's bottle tops tell stories all over the world.

When I started with the aluminum tops I had a small feeling somewhere that it wouldn't last too long. But today, fresh ideas keep coming and I now feel that it's something endless.

EL ANATSUI AND HIS ARTWORK

El Anatsui, 2012.

Woman's Cloth, 2002.

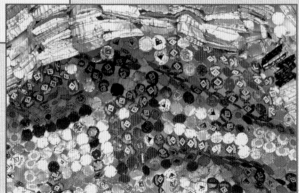

Fresh and Fading Memories, 2007.

AUTHOR'S NOTE

In 1995, I spent a college semester in Ghana. I stayed in Accra near a contemporary art gallery. On the second floor, an unusual sculpture was mounted on the wall. Made from wood and paint, marked and burned, it seemed woven with many ideas, old and new. *Ancient Cloth Series* was my introduction to El's work and I have sought opportunities to see his art ever since.

While El's art was recognized before 2007, the show in Venice was a turning point in his career. In addition to the installation of *Fresh and Fading Memories*, he exhibited two other sculptures at the Biennale (*Dusasa I* and *Dusasa II*) that were widely acclaimed. Today, El's art is shown inside museums and on the outsides of buildings all over the world. Each time the bottle top sculptures are displayed, they are arranged and draped differently.

Some of El's sculptures have names in Ewe, El's first language, like *Gli,* which can mean "wall," "story," or "disrupt," depending on how it is spoken. Some of the names refer to African history.

El finds meaning in the bottles' origins: "Objects such as these were introduced to Africa by Europeans when they came as traders. Alcohol was one of the commodities brought with them to exchange for goods in Africa. Eventually alcohol became one of the items used in the trans-Atlantic slave trade... I thought that the bottle caps had a strong reference to the history of Africa."

El encourages people to view his art and see what it says to them, what it makes them feel. When I look at El's art, I am reminded that art does not require fancy tools or new materials. The things around us can be the raw material for telling our stories, and when we're true to ourselves when we create, the art we make can be powerful and unique.

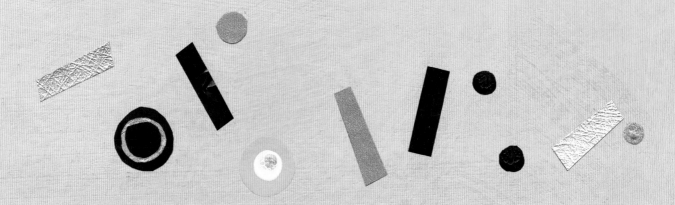

TEXT SOURCES

Anatsui, El. "'Bottle caps are more versatile than canvas and oil': El Anatsui on turning the everyday into art." *The Guardian*, June 21, 2020. https://www.theguardian.com/artanddesign/2020/jun/21/bottle-caps-versatile-el-anatsui-everyday-art.

Anatsui, El and Laura Leffler James. "History, Materials, and the Human Hand—An Interview with El Anatsui." *Art Journal*, Vol. 67, No. 2 (Summer 2008): 36-53.

Art 21. *El Anatsui: Language and Symbols*, 2011. http://www.art21.org/videos/short-el-anatsui-language-symbols.

Bell-Roberts, Brendon. "The Innovation Issue: In Conversation with El Anatsui." *ARTsouthAFRICA*, Vol. 13, No. 3 (March 2015). https://artafricamagazine.org/the-innovation-issue-13-3-a-journey-of-materiality-and-art-practice-in-conversation-with-el-anatsui/.

Binder, Lisa ed. *El Anatsui: When I Last Wrote to You about Africa*. New York: Museum for African Art, 2010.

Brooklyn Museum, *Gravity and Grace: Monumental Works by El Anatsui* (exhibit), February 8–August 18, 2013. www.brooklynmuseum.org/exhibitions/el_anatsui/#!lb_uri=gli.php.

Clark Art Institute. *The installation of El Anatsui's Strips of Earth's Skin* (video), April 2011. www.clarkart.edu/exhibitions/anatsui/content/video-installation.cfm.

El Anatsui's website: www.el-anatsui.com.

Gee, Erika. *El Anatsui: When I Last Wrote to You about Africa, Educator's Guide.* New York: Museum for African Art, 2011.

Gilvin, Amanda and John R. Stromberg eds. *El Anatsui: New Worlds.* Hanover, MA: Mount Holyoke College Art Museum, 2015.

Okafor, Amarachi (assistant and archivist for El Anatsui's studio), correspondence with author, 2021.

Okeke-Agulu, Chika, *El Anatsui at the Clark.* Williamstown, MA: Clark Art Institute, 2011.

Ottenberg, Simon. *New Traditions From Nigeria: Seven Artists of the Nsukka Group.* Washington, DC: Smithsonian Institute Press, 1997.

Picton, John et al. *El Anatsui: A Sculpted History of Africa.* London: Saffron Books, 1998.

Preece, R.J. "El Anatsui Interview: Out of West Africa." Artdesigncafe.com, September 15, 2009. https://www.artdesigncafe.com/el-anatsui-interview-2006.

Princeton Art Museum. "A conversation with El Anatsui" (video), March 26, 2016. https://vimeo.com/180995874.

Smee, Sebastian. "At the Vanguard of a Wave." *The Boston Globe*, April 1, 2011.

Smithsonian National Museum of African Art. *El Anatsui: Gawu* (exhibit website), 2008. africa.si.edu/exhibits/gawu/about.html.

Vogel, Susan Mullin. *El Anatsui: Art and Life.* New York: Prestel, 2012 and 2021.

Vogel, Susan Mullin, and El Anatsui. *Fold Crumple Crush: The Art of El Anatsui.* Brooklyn, NY: Icarus Films, 2011. See also www.susanvogel.com.

QUOTATION SOURCES

p. 9: "We could decide . . . our own terms." Amanda Gilvin and John R. Stromberg eds., *El Anatsui: New Worlds* (Hanover, MA: Mount Holyoke College Art Museum, 2015), p. 39.

p. 10: "School exposed me to . . . my people did." El Anatsui and Laura Leffler James, "History, Materials, and the Human Hand—An Interview with El Anatsui," *Art Journal*, Vol. 67, No. 2 (Summer 2008), p. 43.

p. 13: "The new pot acquires . . . the old pot." *A conversation with El Anatsui* (video), Princeton Art Museum, March 26, 2016 (video), 22:30, viewed at el-anatsui.com. (Also available at: https://vimeo.com/180995874)

p. 14: "If you touch . . . in a way." Susan Vogel, *El Anatsui: Art and Life* (New York: Prestel, 2012), p. 104.

p. 22: "The idea eventually . . . traditional kente cloths." Vogel, *El Anatsui: Art and Life*, p. 54.

p. 30: "When I take . . . three continents." Chika Okeke-Agulu, *El Anatsui at the Clark* (Williamstown, MA: Clark Art Institute, 2011), p. 12.

p. 34: "When I started . . . something endless." Vogel, *El Anatsui: Art and Life*, p. 73.

p. 38: "Objects such as . . . history of Africa." Binder, El Anatsui: When I Last Wrote to You About Africa, p.18

p. 40: "Art grows out . . . environment throws up." Smithsonian National Museum of African Art. *El Anatsui: Gawu*, (exhibit website) https://africa.si.edu/exhibits/gawu/index.html

PHOTO CREDITS

p. 36: Artist El Anatsui, pictured in front of his work *Dzesi II*, 2012, Collection of the Akron Art Museum. Photo by Andrew McAllister

p. 36: El Anatsui, *Woman's Cloth*, 2002. Aluminium and copper wire, 287 x 292 cm. Collection: The Trustees of the British Museum. Photo by Andy Keate. Courtesy the Artist and October Gallery, London.

p. 37: *Fresh and Fading Memories*, Artempo Exhibition, Axel Vervoordt, Palazzo Fortuny. Photo by Jean-Pierre Gabriel.

FEATURED ARTWORK

p. 16: TOP: *Fan*, 1995; RIGHT: *Chip Off the Old Block*, 1991; BOTTOM: *Leopard's Paw-prints and Other Stories*, 1991.

p. 17: *Erosion*, 1992.

pp. 22-23: *Woman's Cloth*, 2002.

pp. 26-27: LEFT: *Man's Cloth*, 2002; RIGHT: *Woman's Cloth*, 2002.

pp. 32-33: *Fresh and Fading Memories*, 2007.

ART ACTIVITY WITH RECYCLED MATERIALS

Art grows out of each particular situation, and I believe that artists are better off working with whatever their environment throws up. —El Anatsui

Many of us come into contact with food wrappers every day. Like El, you can transform used materials into something new. For this activity, collaborate with friends, family members, or classmates to build a sculpture from the foil lids of food containers. Each person can build a patch, which will then join with others to create a large tapestry.

Materials:
- **Foil lids**—Collect the round foil lids from yogurt, applesauce, fruit cups, and other used food containers. Make sure they are clean and dry.
- **Paper clips**—You will use paper clips as fasteners.

Activity:
1. Shape the foil. Fold, pinch, and crush the lids to make a variety of shapes and forms. For example, if you fold the edges of a circle four times you can make a square like El does with the round part of a bottle top. Experiment with the material. The foil lids often have a shiny metal side and a printed side, and you can make different designs by choosing which side of the lids you want to expose.
2. Once you have a number of shapes, fasten them together to create a patch. With help from an adult, carefully pierce the edges of your shapes and loop them together with paper clips. You can bend the paper clips as needed.
3. When each person has completed their patch, spread them all out. Work together to decide how the patches should connect, then join them with more paper clips.
4. Hang the tapestry, step back, and look. Where did the materials come from? Who touched them and left a "charge"? What stories does the artwork tell?